AROUND THE CAMPFIRE

Gerry the Giraffe Goes Camping

Written By
Tom Wach

Illustrated By
Jonny Hossain

Copyright© 2023 by Tom Wach.
All rights reserved.
No part of this book may be reproduced in any written, electronic, recording, or photocopying without written permission of the publisher or author. The exception would be in the case of brief quotations embodied in the critical articles or reviews and pages where permission is specifically granted by the publisher or author.

Dedicated to my two amazing boys, fiancé and family.

Gerry the Giraffe had always been curious about camping and loved spending time outside.

He was always feeling cooped up in the city with no time to relax and explore.

One day, after a lot of planning he gathered all of his gear, packed up his tent and sleeping bag,

and set out on a camping adventure.

He made his way out of the city, through the traffic and onto the highway.

As he looked at all the signs he knew he was getting closer to the campground.

When he arrived, Gerry noticed a group of animals who were amused by his unusual height watching from a distance.

Some of them had never seen a giraffe before. Gerry checked-in and cautiously drove to his campsite nervous about making new friends.

Although he was nervous, Gerry was also excited to go explore and see the beach. With this excitement he headed down to where the others were playing.

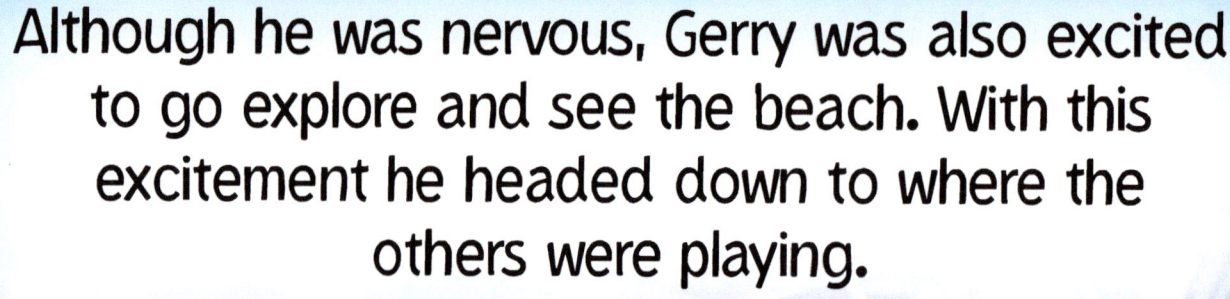

Vanessa saw Gerry sitting by himself and called him over to join. Gerry quickly ran over to build sand castles with his new friends.

The rest of the afternoon was filled with lots of fun swimming, volleyball and a competitive game of hide and seek. Gerry was always the first to be found given his height.

After a long and tiring day at the beach, Gerry made his way back to his campsite.

Having been so excited earlier when he arrived, he realized he hadn't set up his tent or prepared dinner. It was starting to get dark.

Gerry quickly got to work setting up his tent. As soon as he started he noticed all his new friends coming over to help him gather firewood and start a fire.

After his tent was set up and dinner was made it was dark.

Gerry pulled out some flashlights, roasting sticks and marshmallows and asked his new friends to join him. As they sat around the fire they noticed something...

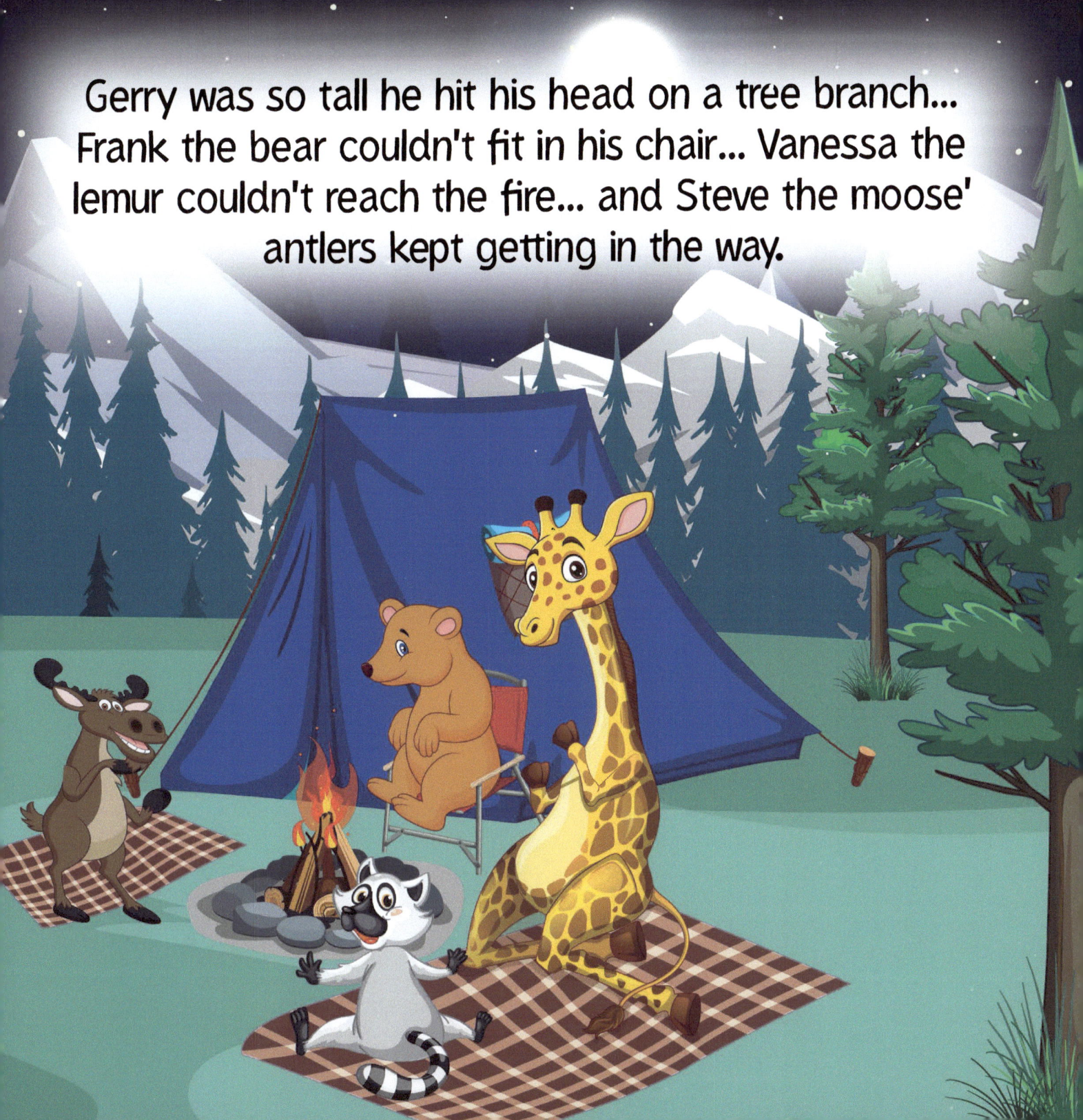

Gerry was so tall he hit his head on a tree branch... Frank the bear couldn't fit in his chair... Vanessa the lemur couldn't reach the fire... and Steve the moose' antlers kept getting in the way.

Although they were all different and all from different places, that night they all became friends.

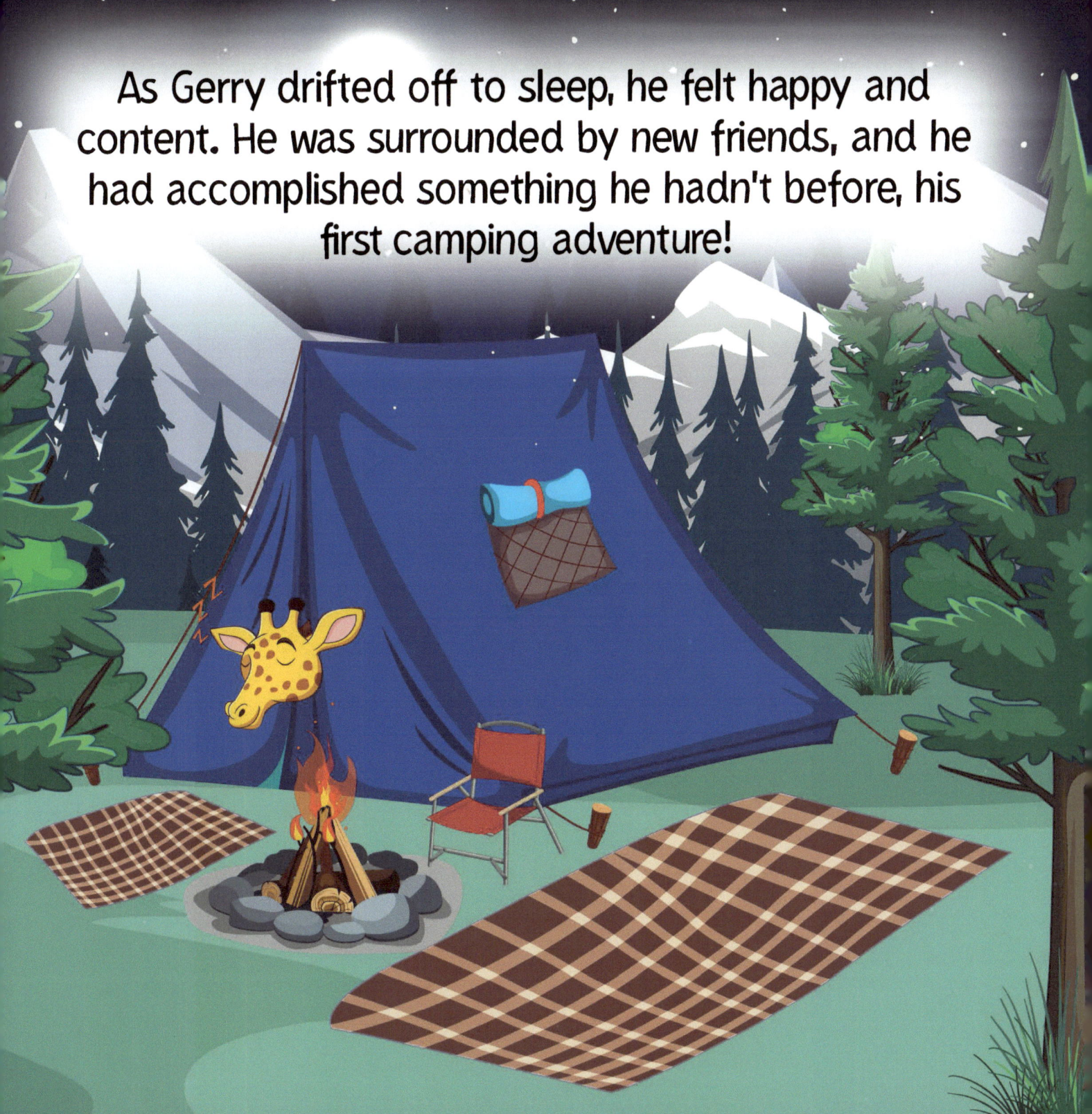

As Gerry drifted off to sleep, he felt happy and content. He was surrounded by new friends, and he had accomplished something he hadn't before, his first camping adventure!

The next morning, as they packed up their gear and said their goodbyes,

As soon as he got back home, Gerry was already planning his next outdoor adventure.